C0-AQR-401

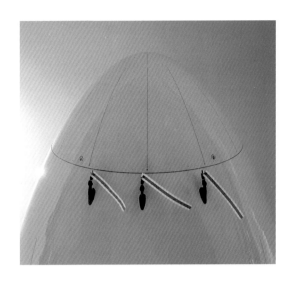

A DAY IN THE LIFE OF **THE FLYING EYE HOSPITAL**

© 2021 Orbis International
Published in 2021 by Orbis International
520 8th Avenue, Suite 1200, New York, NY
10018 USA
www.orbis.org

Nothing contained in this book is to be
considered as the rendering of medical advice
for specific individuals, and readers are
responsible for obtaining such advice from
their own healthcare providers. This book is
intended for educational and informational
purposes only.

All rights reserved. No part of this publication
may be reproduced, distributed, or transmitted
in any form or by any means, including
photocopying, recording, or other electronic
or mechanical methods, without the express
prior written permission of the publisher,
except in the case of brief quotations
embodied in critical reviews. For permission
requests, write to the publisher, addressed
"Attention: Permissions Coordinator," at the
address above.

Orbis, Cybersight, Orbis Flying Eye Hospital,
and Changing the Way the World Sees are all
registered trademarks of Project Orbis
International, Inc.

FedEx is a registered trademark of Federal
Express Corporation. Used with permission.

OMEGA is a registered trademark of Omega
Ltd. Used with permission.

ISBN 978-0-578-85500-4
Photography: Nick Wood
Photographs on pages 2-11, 111, back cover:
Geoff Oliver Bugbee
Design: Clare Baggaley
Illustrations on pages 10 and 11: Pause for
Thought
Flags: www.flaticon.com
Contributors: Louise Harris, Kristin Taylor,
Isabelle Tietbohl
Printed by: Everbest Printing Investment
Limited with thanks to Ian Lambot

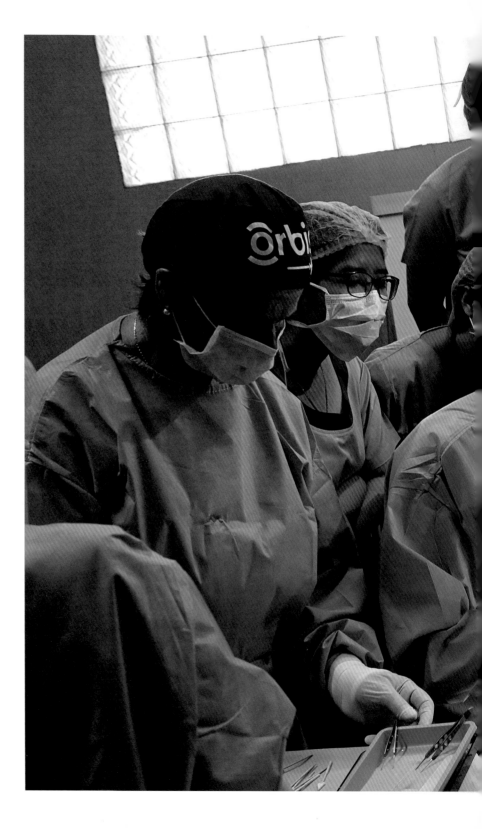

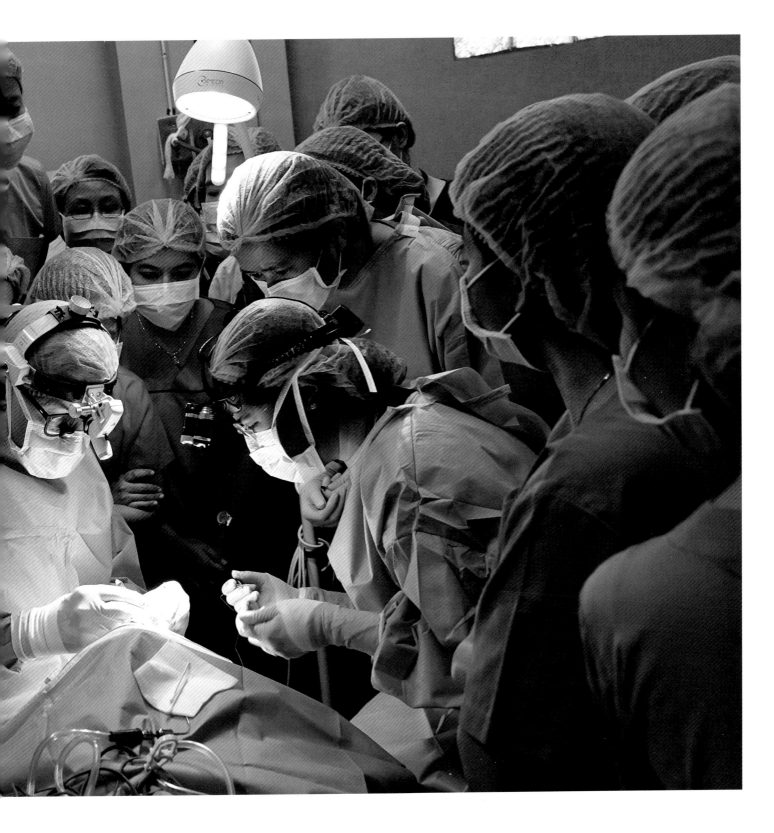

CHANGING THE WAY
THE WORLD SEES

Imagine losing your sight somewhere in the world with little or no access to eye care. Where would you turn for help? With few quality eye doctors, hospitals or clinics, your chances of getting the right kind of care would be small. As your sight got worse, your chances of getting an education or earning a steady income would also become smaller and smaller. This is the reality for millions of people living in low- and middle-income countries, home to 90% of people with vision loss.

Orbis knows that the only way to make a real difference is to build solutions that will go the distance and ensure people can receive quality eye care when and where they need it. Alongside a network of partners, Orbis works to mentor, train and inspire local teams so that they can provide quality eye care in their communities. It's the "teach a person to fish" model. We put an emphasis on training local eye care teams – from community health workers to anesthesiologists, from eye surgeons to nurses – so that they can work together to restore sight.

Our mission at Orbis is to transform lives through the prevention and treatment of blindness. We envision a world where no one loses their sight due to a lack of care. None of this work would be possible without the generous support of our donors.

ORBIS:
IT'S ALL ABOUT SIGHT

Globally, 1.1 billion people live with vision loss, and a staggering 90% of it could be completely avoided. Often something as simple as getting a routine cataract surgery or a pair of glasses is all that is needed to restore a person's vision.

Great strides are being made in increasing access to eye care, but needs are still urgent and rapidly growing. As people live longer lives, as the world's population grows and as lifestyle changes cause an uptick in conditions like diabetic retinopathy, we are seeing an increasing number of people with sight-threatening conditions who need eye care.

The most effective, lasting solution to these challenges is to ensure that eye care professionals everywhere can access ophthalmic training, building the skills they need to provide quality eye care to patients in their communities.

WHAT WE DO

We fight avoidable blindness in low- and middle-income countries around the world, tailoring our work to meet the needs of local communities. We carry out our mission in a number of ways. Our Flying Eye Hospital is the world's only fully accredited ophthalmic teaching hospital on board an MD-10 plane. We have 400 world-class medical volunteers from more than 30 countries – our "Volunteer Faculty" – who donate their time and expertise to train and mentor other eye care professionals. Hospital-based trainings grow the skills of eye care professionals in the facilities where they work. Our long-term country programs build and strengthen eye health systems with the help of our staff at permanent offices and other local partners around the world. Our award-winning telemedicine platform, Cybersight, is the largest online resource in the world for ophthalmic training. We use Cybersight to provide education, professional mentoring and patient care consultation to eye care professionals around the world. This is especially important for places that are harder to reach, including geographically isolated communities or conflict-affected areas.

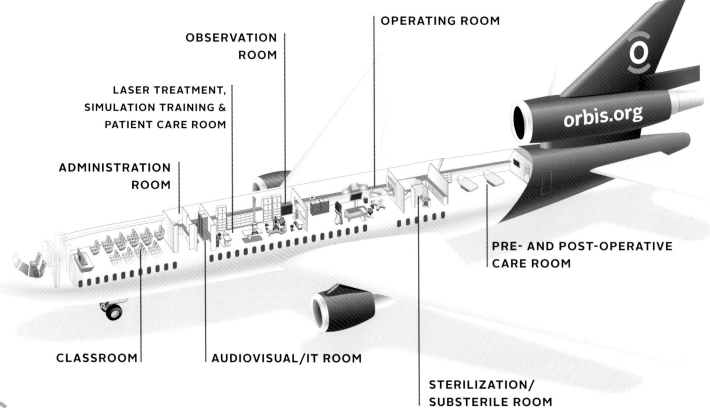

OPERATING ROOM

OBSERVATION ROOM

LASER TREATMENT, SIMULATION TRAINING & PATIENT CARE ROOM

ADMINISTRATION ROOM

orbis.org

PRE- AND POST-OPERATIVE CARE ROOM

CLASSROOM

AUDIOVISUAL/IT ROOM

STERILIZATION/ SUBSTERILE ROOM

WHERE WE WORK

Orbis came about through a unique and lasting alliance between aviation and medicine. Our founder, ophthalmologist Dr. David Paton, observed a severe lack of eye care in low- and middle-income countries, where blindness was widespread. The high costs of tuition and international travel prevented most eye care professionals in these areas from getting quality training. Dr. Paton believed that bringing training where it was needed most would allow local eye care teams to build the skills to provide quality eye care in their communities. Thus, the idea of outfitting an aircraft with an ophthalmic teaching hospital was born and, with it, Orbis and our Flying Eye Hospital.

Orbis – Latin for "of the eye" and Greek for "around the world" – encapsulates Dr. Paton's novel vision. Since our Flying Eye Hospital took its first flight in 1982, it has visited more than 95 countries, offering world-class ophthalmic training to eye care professionals who urgently need it. Today, Orbis continues to focus our efforts in low- and middle-income countries, home to 90% of people with vision loss.

OUR GLOBAL REACH & IMPACT

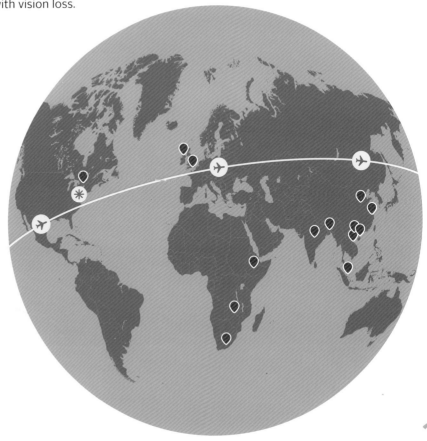

✈ **97** countries visited by the Flying Eye Hospital since 1982

⬤ **14** fundraising and program offices around the world

✳ **1** headquarters in New York

MEET OUR AMAZING TEAM

BRUCE JOHNSON

MAURICE GEARY

CAPTAIN CYNDHI BERWYN

DR. ANTONIO JARAMILLO

DR. PETER MOORE

SOLOMON ABERRA

SANDY BURNETT

RONALD GYI

DR. OMAR SALAMANCA

ELISA URRUCHI

KIMBERLY McQUAID

JACQUELINE NEWTON

The Flying Eye Hospital team is made up of very special staff and volunteers from all corners of the globe – Africa, Asia, Australia, the Caribbean, Europe, Latin America and North America.

This is a truly multi-national, multicultural team that shares one thing in common: a passion for saving sight. Learn about some of them here and the incredible work that they do.

DR. ANDREAS DI LUCIANO

JANGAIAH CHALAMALA

CELIA YEUNG

ANGELA PURCELL

STAN LOVIN

DR. SANDRA JOHNSON

DR. MARIA MONTERO

VALERIE SUBERG

LEO MERCADO

DR. BRADFORD LEE

ALANA CALISE

GLORIA RHOOMES-MUSHORE

BRUCE JOHNSON

DIRECTOR, AIRCRAFT OPERATIONS, USA

ABOVE: Tubes connect to the front of the plane to provide air conditioning.

"We can have as many as 15 different nationalities working at the same time together, and it works because we are all here for the same cause."

Bruce and his team are responsible for all aviation aspects of the Flying Eye Hospital, making sure the entire operation stays safe and efficient. Bruce is deeply familiar with every part of the plane, down to the very last rivet.

Every day is different for Bruce, whether it's working on the flight plan for the next Orbis program, managing a regular maintenance check or negotiating with local airport authorities for every aspect required to land and operate safely in the local country.

This aircraft is the third-generation Flying Eye Hospital, an MD-10 donated by FedEx. The first Flying Eye Hospital, a DC-8, took off in 1982, and since that time, our plane has flown to over 95 countries to save and restore sight.

ABOVE Bruce and Captain Cyndhi Berwyn finalize a pre-flight check before the plane takes off.

TOP Bruce Johnson in front of the Flying Eye Hospital before it takes off.

LEFT A bolt on the wheel of the plane is painted yellow to indicate that it is a specially made piece.

THE MD-10 HAS A WINGSPAN OF 165 FEET. THAT'S TALLER THAN A 15-STORY BUILDING!

MAURICE GEARY

DIRECTOR, FLYING EYE HOSPITAL, IRELAND

ABOVE Maurice sits in the classroom of the Flying Eye Hospital and listens to a lecture.

"I met a patient in Peru who had her sight restored on an Orbis program. Both her husband and daughter are blind, and without the sight-saving surgery she received, she would not have been able to care for her family."

As the Director of the Flying Eye Hospital, Maurice leads a dynamic team of eye health and NGO professionals dedicated to bringing medical education and treatment programs to partner hospitals worldwide. He works closely with every part of the team, from the flight mechanics to our staff nurses.

He is responsible for the smooth running of every Flying Eye Hospital program. This includes visiting countries well before the plane lands and assessing the program after it leaves.

LEFT Maurice helps to make sure each Flying Eye Hospital program runs smoothly, and even begins planning a year in advance.

RIGHT Maurice observes preparation for surgery happening at a local hospital in Jamaica.

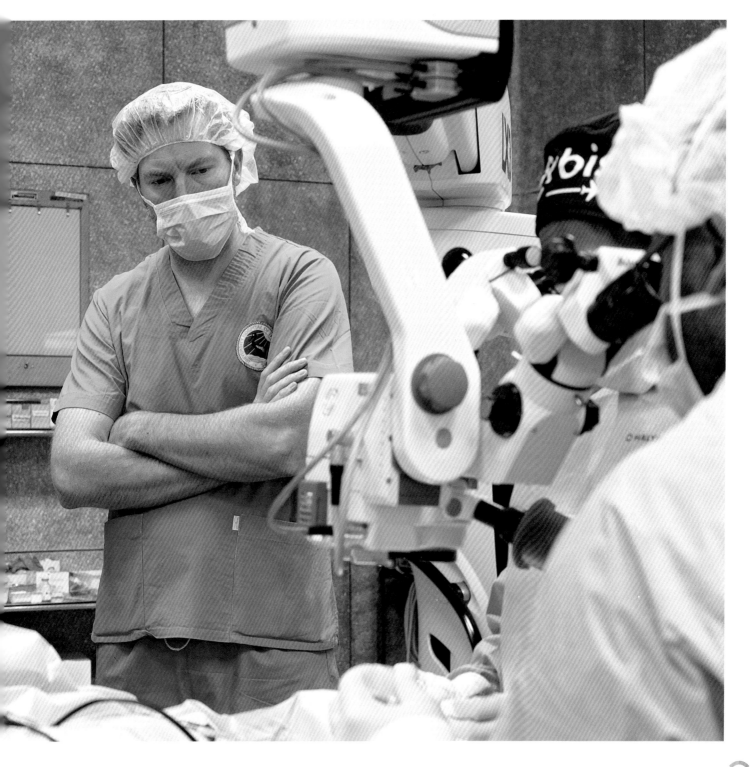

CAPTAIN CYNDHI BERWYN

PILOT, USA

ABOVE Cyndhi stands in the cockpit after finishing a pre-flight check.

"It is so rewarding to be a part of something bigger than yourself, and it touches me every time someone is gifted with sight."

Orbis wouldn't be able to carry out its sight-saving work without people like Captain Cyndhi Berwyn, one of 18 incredible FedEx pilots who volunteer their time to fly the plane – officially known as Orbis 1 – to its next destination.

For pilots, the aircraft provides a unique experience – they meet children who can't see one day then get their vision back a few days later. When she's not flying Orbis 1, you'll find Cyndhi training other FedEx pilots in her role as senior manager of flight training.

RIGHT Pictured here is the cockpit of the MD-10, which is completely digital.

THE MD-10 CAN FLY UP TO 6,000 NAUTICAL MILES.

DR. ANTONIO JARAMILLO

HEAD OF CLINICAL SERVICES, COLOMBIA

ABOVE Antonio looks on as an Orbis staff nurse trains a local nurse in preparing for surgery.

"I treated a boy in Cameroon for strabismus. He and his father came back for post-operative care, and his dad was wearing a soccer jersey from my home country of Colombia to show his appreciation. It was such a special moment."

Antonio supervises all clinical activities on board the Flying Eye Hospital. He is responsible for keeping all Orbis policies and records updated to ensure that the plane maintains its accreditation through AAAASFI as an ambulatory surgical facility. As an ophthalmologist, Antonio oversees all of the operations and surgical planning on board the Flying Eye Hospital as well as at local hospitals.

The Orbis Flying Eye Hospital is the only accredited hospital on board an aircraft. In order to make sure the Flying Eye Hospital keeps this accreditation, Antonio must monitor all surgeries and pre- and post-operative care to ensure that the highest standards are being met. Meeting these standards of medical care and equipment enables us to deliver the highest quality training and patient care.

THE FLYING EYE HOSPITAL IS ACCREDITED BY THE AMERICAN ASSOCIATION FOR ACCREDITATION OF AMBULATORY SURGERY FACILITIES INTERNATIONAL (AAAASFI), MAKING IT **THE ONLY NON-LAND-BASED HOSPITAL TO ACHIEVE THIS STANDARD.**

— WITH OUR DEEP GRATITUDE —

A.C. Uebschi
Abundant Grace Charity Foundation Ltd
Alcon Foundation
The Bliss Family Charity
The Boeing Company
Carl Zeiss Meditec, Inc.
Creative Electronics, Inc.
Cognacy Foundation
The Eye Surgery Fund
FedEx Express
GE Aviation
Ho Man Fat Memorial Foundation
Jebsen Group
LOCCITANE en Provence

LIFT Strategic Design

Mrs. Grace Tsao

Ms. Ho Cheuk Wai Salina &
Ms. Ho Cheuk Chi Susanna

Ms. Lei Ioc Heng

Mrs. Thomas S. Knight, Jr.

NOVA VISION 星创视界

Omni Air International

TrueVision Systems

United Airlines

Vivienne Poy

Yuen Yee Charity Found

Zodiac Aerospac

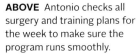

ABOVE Antonio checks all surgery and training plans for the week to make sure the program runs smoothly.

RIGHT Antonio oversees training activities happening on board the Flying Eye Hospital.

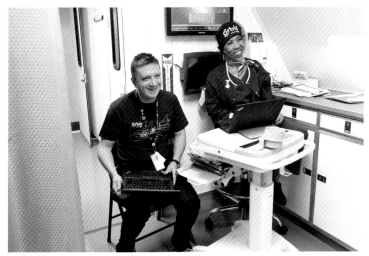

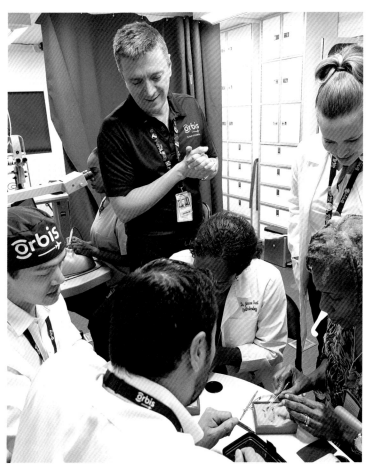

DR. PETER MOORE

ANESTHESIOLOGIST, AUSTRALIA

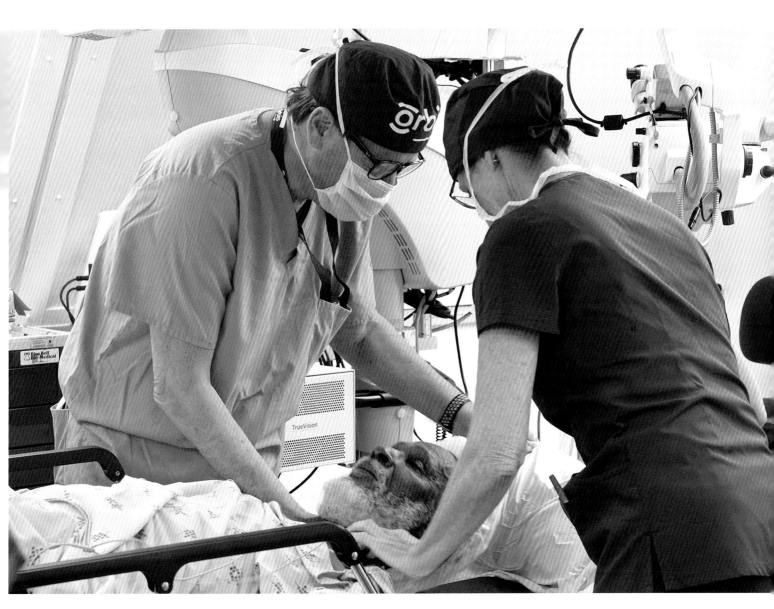

ABOVE Peter preps the anesthesia for a patient about to undergo cataract surgery.

"In Peru, I remember how nervous a young boy was before his eye surgery until we brought out a model airplane for him to play with. One simple gesture like this can make a huge difference in making a patient feel safe."

Many surgeries to prevent and treat avoidable blindness – such as cataract surgery – can be performed on adults using local anesthetic. That's not the case with young children, who need to have general anesthesia to correct problems like cataracts or strabismus. Teaching safe practices in anesthesia is a vital part of Orbis training, and Peter shares his skills with local teams in the operating room. Part of the training involves simulation on a manikin called a Pediasim, allowing local anesthesiologists to learn how to respond to emergency situations that may arise in their hospitals.

ABOVE Going over the anesthesia plan is a critical part of preparing a patient for surgery.

RIGHT Peter monitors the vitals of a patient during surgery to ensure everything is running smoothly.

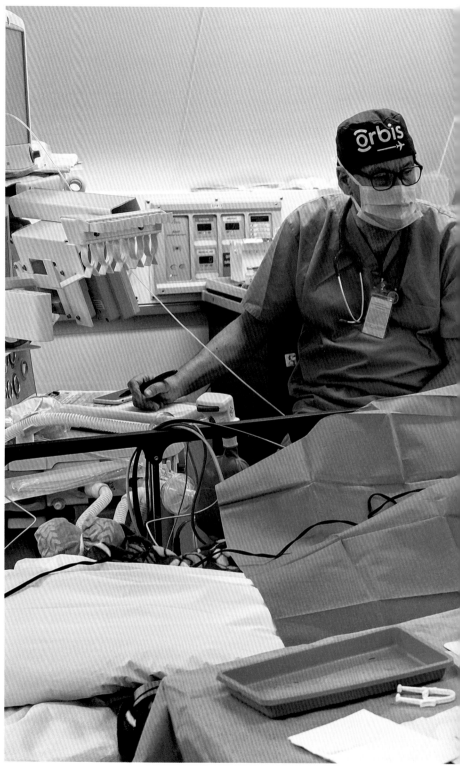

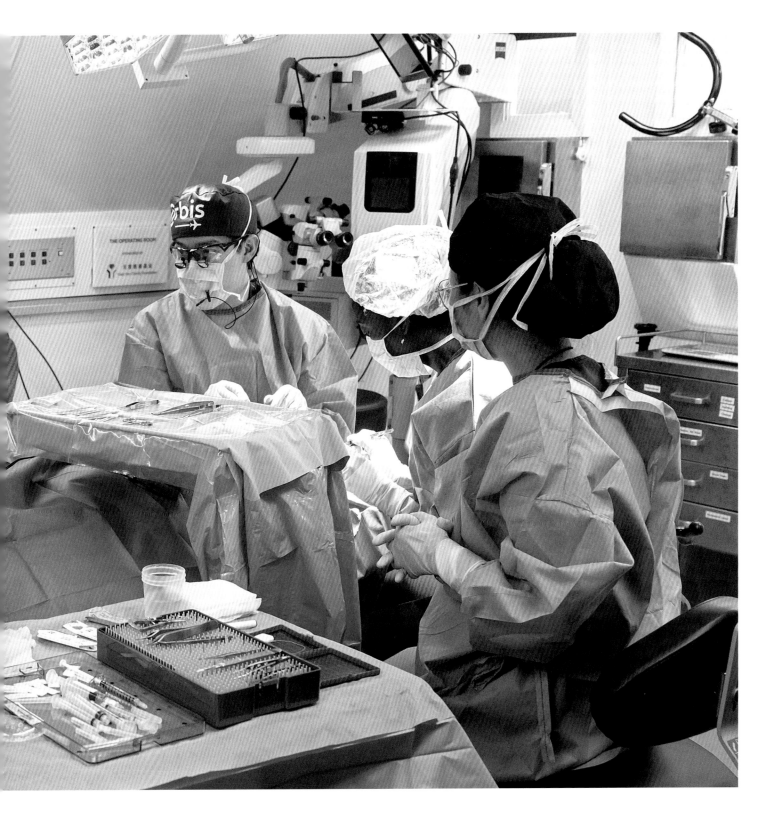

SOLOMON ABERRA

SENIOR MANAGER, LOGISTICS & ADMINISTRATION, ETHIOPIA

ABOVE Solomon works with local airport staff to ensure that doctors, patients and family members are all accounted for.

"There are so many small moving parts that are critical to ensuring the success of our mission."

Solomon works to plan, coordinate and manage all of the logistics that go into each Flying Eye Hospital program. This includes oversight of the safety and security of our team and participants, coordinating and assisting with travel, immigration and customs, managing the supplies required by the team, the packing and unpacking of the plane and supporting the audiovisual and IT teams.

Solomon is responsible for making sure all staff, participants and visitors adhere to plans and scheduling. His job requires a lot of active problem-solving. He must handle complex situations and multiple responsibilities simultaneously, mixing long-term needs with the urgency of immediate demands.

LEFT Arranging transport to and from the Flying Eye Hospital is a critical part of delivering training to local eye care teams.

TOP Doctors, nurses and Orbis staff all arrive safely and on time to the Flying Eye Hospital.

LEFT Solomon works closely with all members of the Orbis team to ensure everything runs smoothly.

OUR AMAZING SUPPORTERS, VOLUNTEERS AND PARTNERS ARE AT THE HEART OF EVERYTHING WE DO.

SANDY BURNETT

VOLUNTEER FACULTY, NURSE, USA

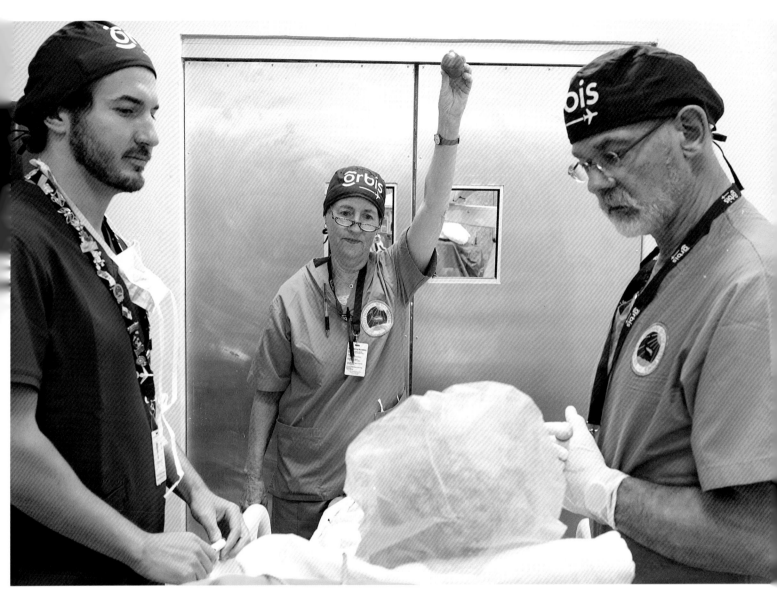

ABOVE Sandy shows local nurses how she makes sure patients feel comfortable and safe before going into surgery.

"I helped care for a 7-year-old child in Peru with a traumatic eye injury. Twenty-seven years later, he was on board the Flying Eye Hospital again for a different eye condition. His mother hugged me when she realized I was part of the team that saved her son's sight all those years ago."

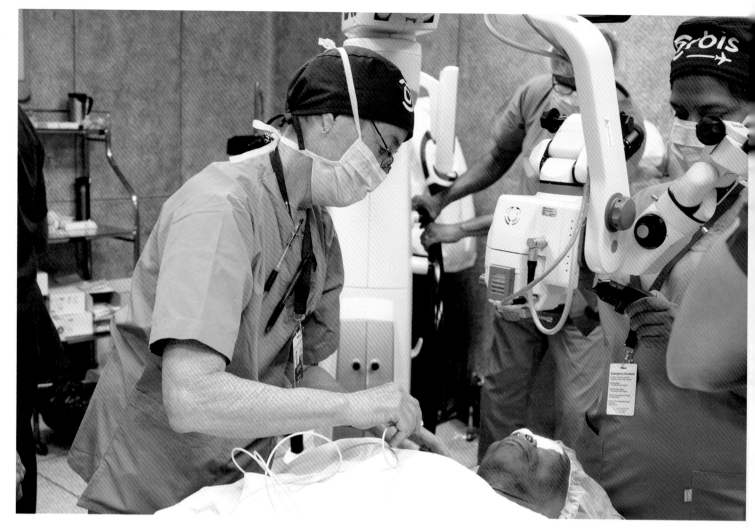

NURSES PLAY A CRITICAL ROLE IN PREVENTING COMPLICATIONS DURING SURGERY, AND ENSURING POSITIVE OUTCOMES FOR PATIENTS OVERALL.

TOP Nurse Sandy attaches heart rate monitors to a patient before she undergoes surgery.

RIGHT Nurse Sandy administers eye drops before a patient has her eyes examined.

ABOVE Nurse Sandy meets with a patient from Jamaica who will undergo eye surgery the next day.

Sandy is one of our incredible Volunteer Faculty members, working as a nurse on our programs. She teaches colleagues around the world how to deliver quality care to patients and their families.

One of Sandy's personal techniques is to establish a cheerful, caring style of nursing that engages the patient and makes them feel comfortable, safe and respected. This allows them to have confidence with her skills as a nurse. In turn, it also leads to more positive outcomes, including better patient cooperation, reduced anxiety and improved healing. Sharing this skill set with fellow ophthalmic nurses teaches them a diversified approach to care that can be useful in their community.

RONALD GYI

BIOMEDICAL ENGINEER, MYANMAR

ABOVE Ronald monitors a microscope equipped with a 3D lens before surgery begins.

"One of the most important parts of our programs is the training, and it's critical to train every level of the medical team in the countries where we work. I get to work with the biomedical engineers and make sure they know how to fix and maintain the equipment that is so crucial to sight-saving surgeries."

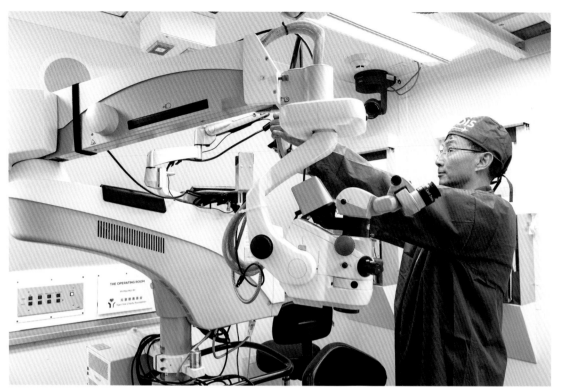

Taking care of high-tech medical equipment and ensuring it works well in a precise medical field such as ophthalmology requires special expertise. On board the Flying Eye Hospital, you'll find a laser room and simulation center packed with machines such as surgical simulators and virtual reality devices; these are used to teach techniques to local doctors in a safe way before they operate on patients. Ronald not only maintains this equipment, but also teaches other biomedical engineers to manage and maintain the equipment that they have in their local hospitals.

TOP Ronald checks the microscope used for surgery on the Flying Eye Hospital. During surgery, a camera in the microscope broadcasts a 3D view of the operation to eye care teams in the plane's classroom.

LEFT Ronald trains local biomedical engineers on how to maintain the simulation equipment used for ophthalmic training.

TOP Ronald checks equipment used to train eye care professionals on board the Flying Eye Hospital.

LEFT Orbis has state-of-the-art equipment for monitoring the administration of anesthesia.

BIOMEDICAL ENGINEERS ARE RESPONSIBLE FOR MAINTAINING AND MONITORING EQUIPMENT THAT'S CRITICAL TO SAVING SIGHT.

DR. OMAR SALAMANCA

STAFF OPHTHALMOLOGIST, COLOMBIA

ABOVE Omar stands outside a local hospital as patients wait to have their eyes examined.

"Weeks after finishing the program, when I perform the surgical case review, I find that the patients we have operated on are very pleased with the results of the surgeries; they have improved their vision, and they describe to me how their life has changed."

Omar's role is to design the ophthalmology training projects that will be delivered in each program; they are based on the needs identified in planning visits that take place long before the Flying Eye Hospital arrives in a country.

Once a program has begun, Omar coordinates all medical and surgical activities. He also participates in the training of local ophthalmologists, especially in the area of glaucoma. You can often find Omar training local eye care teams using simulation technology, such as artificial eyes, life-like manikins and virtual reality simulators, which help local teams practice their surgical skills and detect various eye diseases. This new technology allows local ophthalmology teams to learn complex skills in a controlled environment before operating on a patient.

TOP Omar demonstrates how to use a training device known as the EyeSi to practice surgical skills.

BOTTOM Omar goes over the clinical schedule for the day with all members of the Orbis team.

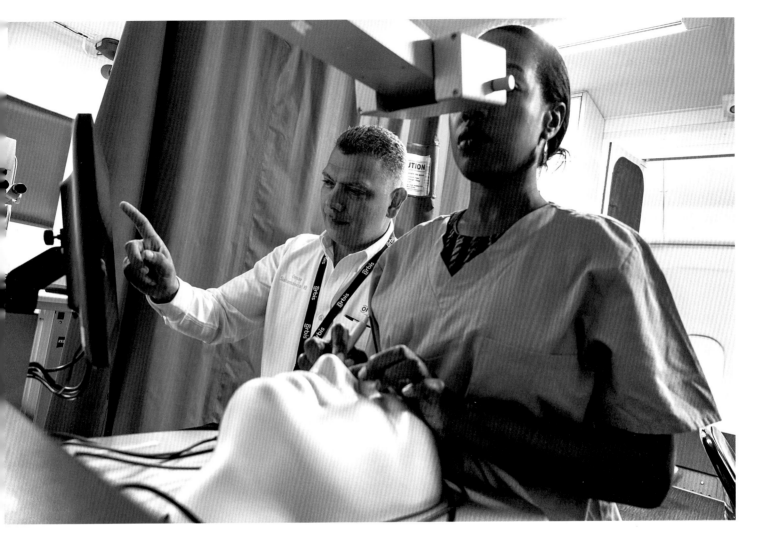

TOP Omar trains a local doctor who is building her skills using a virtual reality simulator.

LEFT Omar answers questions as training participants in the Flying Eye Hospital's classroom watch the live stream of a surgery taking place in the plane's operating room.

ELISA URRUCHI

STAFF NURSE, PERU

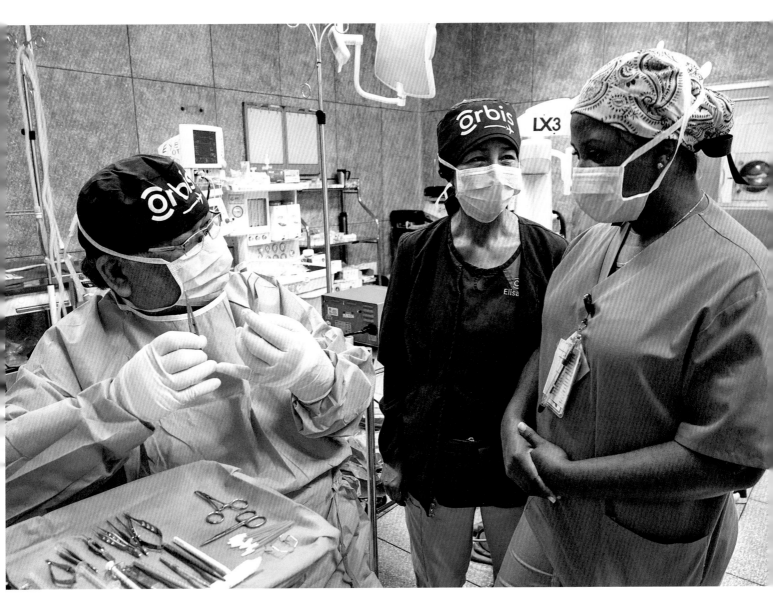

ABOVE Elisa reviews with a local nurse the process for sterilizing and preparing equipment for surgery.

"I helped correct strabismus on a 70-year-old patient in Peru. This man had to suffer for years with a condition that could've been corrected during his childhood if he'd had access to proper care."

Elisa's main role is to train nurses in the countries where Orbis works. This training can be during the Flying Eye Hospital programs or during hospital-based trainings.

One of many unique things about the Flying Eye Hospital is that it has its own water-purification system. This helps manage infection control in surgeries and operations. These techniques are also taught in local hospitals.

In Ethiopia, infection control is especially critical in eradicating trachoma, a highly contagious infectious disease that causes blindness. There, Orbis incorporates into its trainings a strategy known as SAFE, which includes surgery for trichiasis, an advanced stage of trachoma; distribution of antibiotics; and education on the importance of good sanitation and hygiene practices.

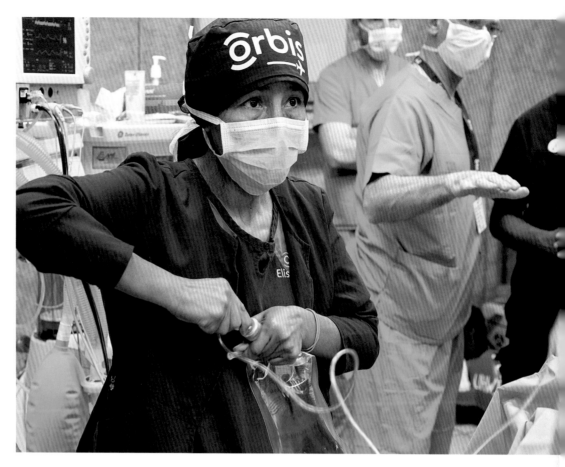

TOP Elisa prepares anesthesia equipment before surgery.

RIGHT Members of the surgical team go over their responsibilities before entering the operating room.

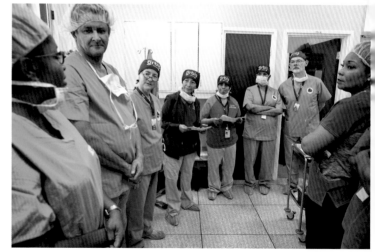

**GLOBALLY, 90%
OF VISION LOSS IS
PREVENTABLE OR
TREATABLE.**

KIMBERLY McQUAID

ALLIED HEALTH TECHNICIAN, USA

ABOVE Kimberly walks through eye examination techniques with a local technician.

"One of the most heartfelt moments I have experienced with Orbis was when, one final day of a program, my trainee looked to me and said, 'Kim, I love you, and I don't want you to leave.' I knew she had gained a lot during my time with her, and her genuine affection and gratitude were the ultimate reward."

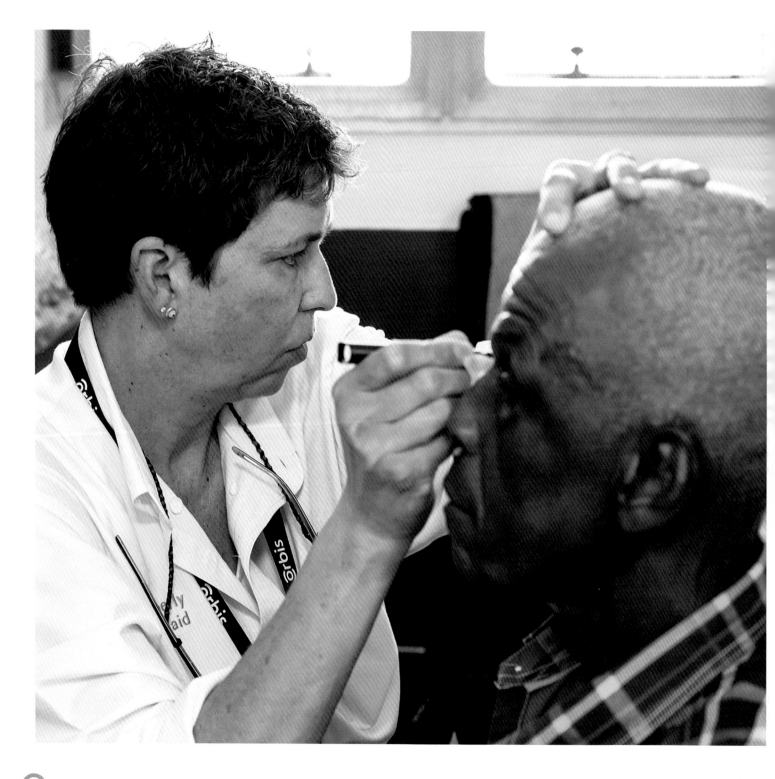

As the Allied Health Technician for the Flying Eye Hospital, Kimberly teaches ophthalmic officers, technicians, nurses and resident ophthalmologists everything from basic skills to the finer points of complex diagnostic testing. These eye care professionals often serve as a direct link between the patient and the doctor. Improving their ability and level of understanding leads to better patient outcomes. Kim always hopes the people she trains will apply their newfound skills to their own practice and will be able to effectively teach their colleagues. Her favorite part is seeing that "lightbulb moment" when she has provided a connection for them between one thing and another. She tries to instill in them the importance of their role and pride in the responsibility they have to take care of patients and each other.

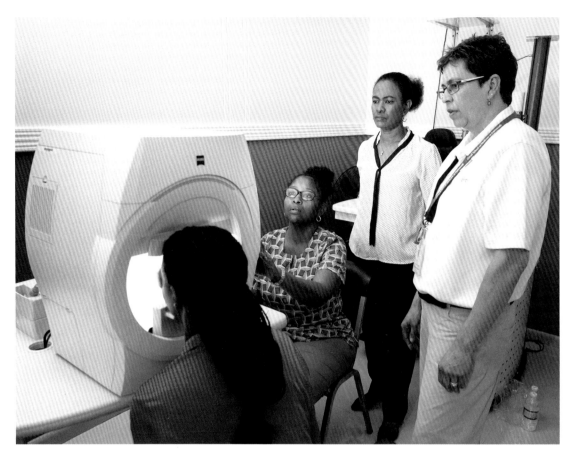

RIGHT Kimberly trains local technicians on how to use advanced eye-screening equipment.

LEFT Kimberly examines a patient's eyes.

JACQUELINE NEWTON

STAFF NURSE, SOUTH AFRICA

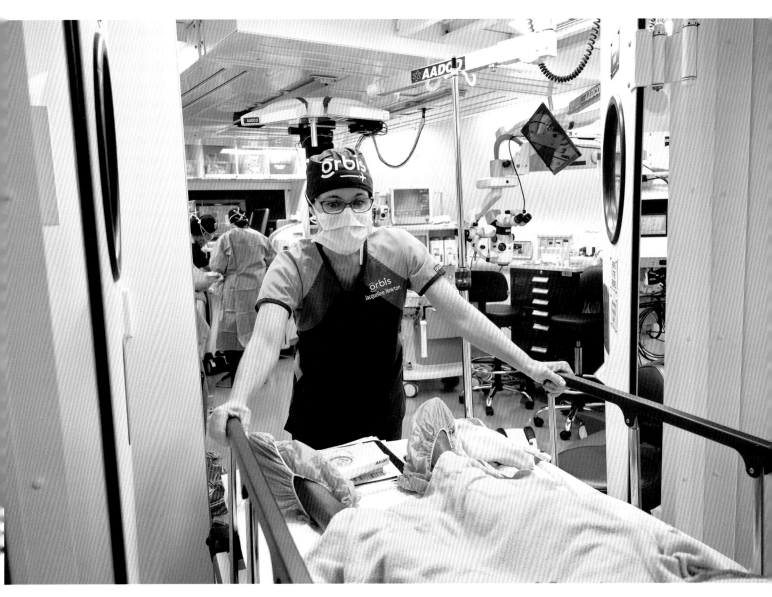

ABOVE Jacqueline brings a patient into the operating room on board the Flying Eye Hospital.

"I still remember my first day with Orbis, in Tanzania. It made me realize I found my purpose, and I felt like I was exactly where I was meant to be."

ORBIS'S WORK IS COMPLETELY **FUNDED BY DONATIONS.**

TOP Jacqueline trains local nurses on how to provide the highest quality care for their patients.

RIGHT Jacqueline joins a team briefing before patients are screened at a local clinic.

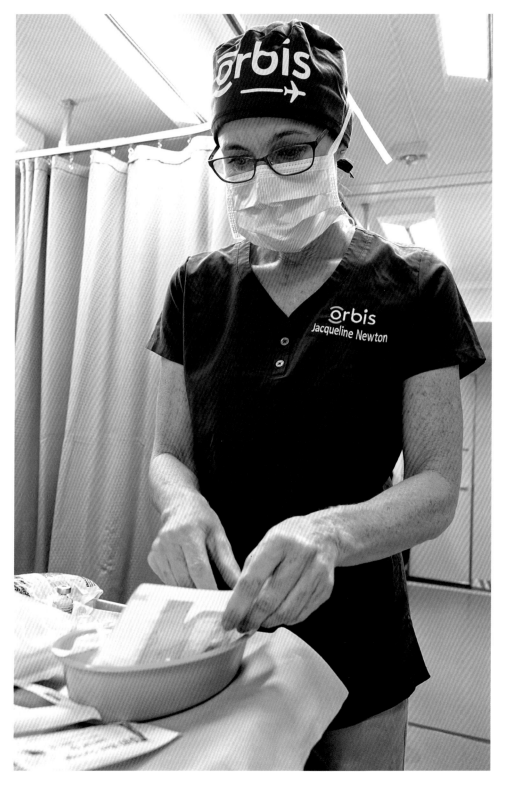

As a staff nurse, Jacqueline works alongside nurses from local hospitals and shares best practices in areas such as preparing patients for surgery, assisting in their recovery, helping surgeons during operations, properly cleaning and sterilizing surgical instruments and ensuring the highest quality of patient care.

Jacqueline and fellow nurses also assist in the operating room. They create an environment where local teams receive training on how to prepare patients for surgery and monitor them during an operation.

RIGHT Jacqueline ensures that all equipment needed for surgery is properly sterlized and prepared.

DR. ANDREAS DI LUCIANO

STAFF OPHTHALMOLOGIST, CHILE

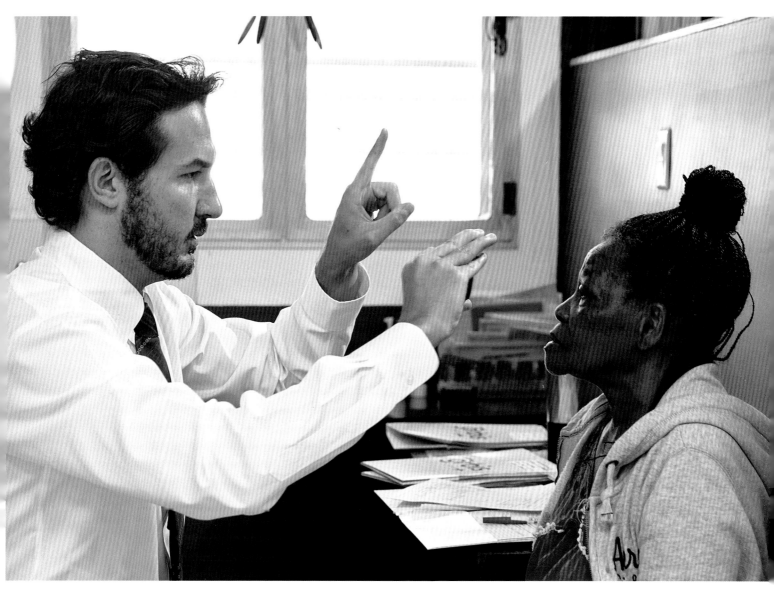

ABOVE Andreas completes an eye exam at a local hospital.

"I love to see how happy our beautiful patients are after they regain their sight."

As one of the Orbis staff ophthalmologists, Dr. Andreas di Luciano works side by side with the teams on the Flying Eye Hospital as well as in local hospitals to ensure the smooth running and success of an Orbis program.

An Orbis program takes up to 18 months of planning before it begins, and our staff ophthalmologists play a key role. When a program starts, you'll find Andreas screening patients in the local hospital, teaching the local medical team and taking care of patients to make them feel comfortable.

When patients receive ophthalmological care on an Orbis program, we turn it into an opportunity to teach local eye care teams how to deliver the same care in their community. With more skilled teams, more people can live lives free from avoidable blindness.

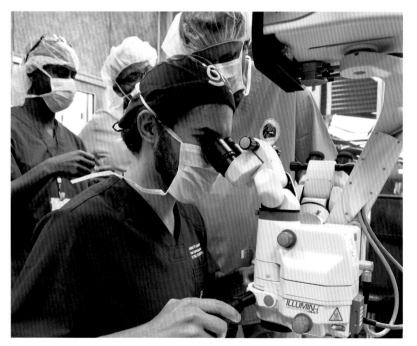

TOP Andreas goes over pre-surgery forms with members of the Orbis team.

BOTTOM Andreas looks into a microscope in a local hospital in Jamaica.

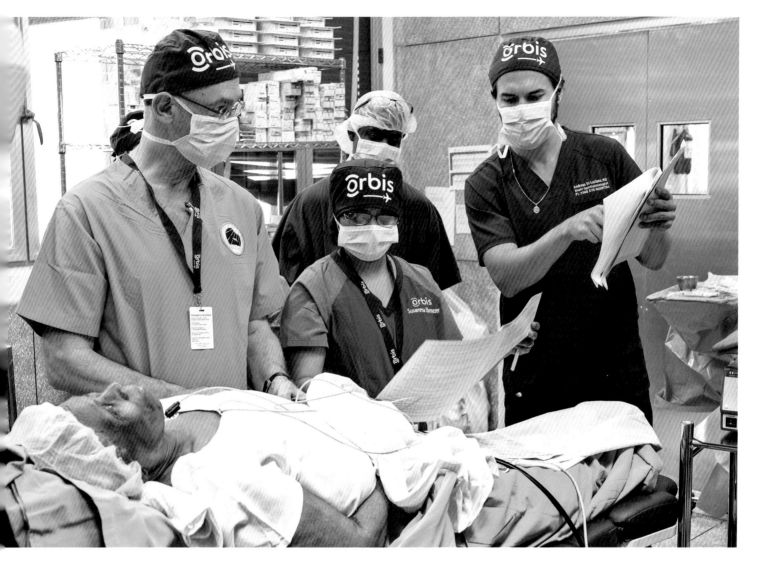

EVERY $1 INVESTED IN EYE HEALTH IN LOW- AND MIDDLE-INCOME COUNTRIES IS ESTIMATED TO YIELD $4 IN ECONOMIC GAIN.

ABOVE Andreas works closely with all members of the medical team to ensure patients are safe and ready for surgery.

JANGAIAH CHALAMALA

AUDIOVISUAL SPECIALIST, INDIA

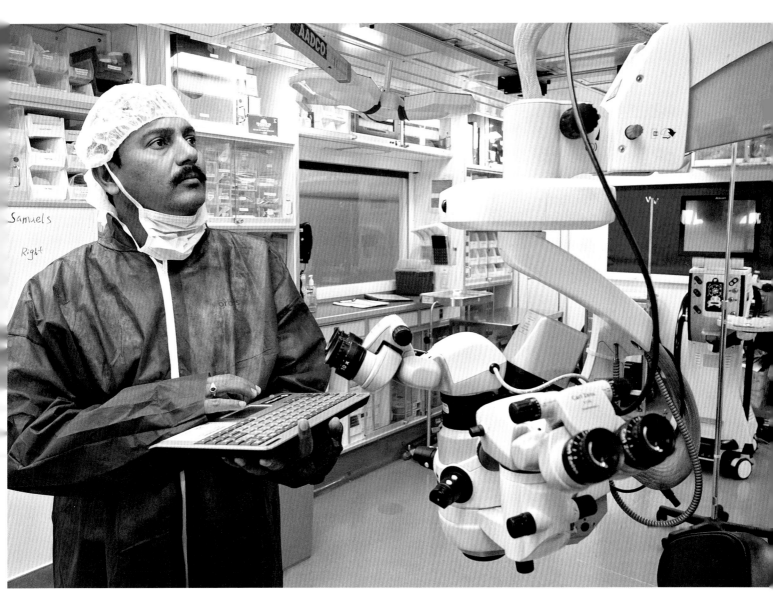

ABOVE Jangaiah ensures that all cameras in the operating room's microscope are working so that surgeries can be broadcast to the Flying Eye Hospital's classroom and to eye care professionals around the world via our telemedicine platform, Cybersight.

"I am so grateful for all of the moments working with Orbis. We all come together from across the world for the same goal."

Jangaiah serves as one of our audiovisual specialists, managing all of the broadcast capabilities on board the plane. His command center is the audiovisual room, where he controls the cameras that are in every part of the plane.

Video from a unique 3D camera system built into the microscope in the operating room allows the surgeries to be broadcast into the classroom at the front of plane; participants feel as if they are also looking down the microscope. A two-way microphone allows them to ask the lead surgeon questions in real time. These surgeries are also broadcast on our telemedicine platform, Cybersight.

ALL Jangaiah helps to monitor the feed of 16 cameras mounted throughout the plane to ensure all training activities can be broadcast in the classroom and on Cybersight.

THERE ARE A TOTAL OF 16 CAMERAS MOUNTED THROUGHOUT THE PLANE.

CELIA YEUNG

COMMUNICATIONS MANAGER, HONG KONG

ABOVE Celia leads a tour of the Flying Eye Hospital for FedEx employees.

"It's a lot of hard work and long hours, but it's a really unique environment. We can have up to 25 staff and 12 volunteers on board from over 20 different nations, so it's like working in a mini-United Nations!"

As the Communications Manager, Celia is responsible for all the PR, media, public awareness and advocacy campaigns of the Flying Eye Hospital, wherever it goes. The Flying Eye Hospital has been described as a teacher and an envoy since it grabs attention whenever it lands in a country. Celia proudly introduces the plane and hosts tours for heads of state, prime ministers, ministers of health, ambassadors, celebrities and media to promote Orbis's work and raise awareness of the prevention and treatment of blindness around the world.

LEFT Celia leads a tour of the Flying Eye Hospital.

RIGHT Celia walks guests through the plane's simulation training center and classroom.

ANGELA PURCELL

HEAD NURSE, JAMAICA & UNITED KINGDOM

ABOVE Angela trains local nurses in post-operative care.

"It's very gratifying to know that I can play a role in the prevention of blindness."

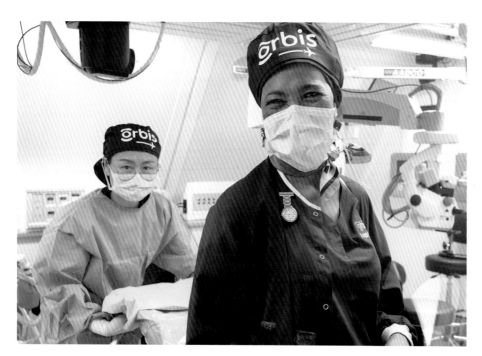

TOP LEFT Angela smiles as another patient's sight is restored on board the Flying Eye Hospital.

BOTTOM LEFT Angela explains the importance of sterilization and infection control in the post-operative care room.

RIGHT Angela holds a teddy bear in the pre- and post-operative care room. OMEGA donates these bears to comfort children who have undergone surgery.

NURSES ARE OFTEN PATIENTS' FIRST LINE OF CONTACT FOR UNDERSTANDING THE PROCEDURE THEY ARE ABOUT TO UNDERGO, AS WELL AS THEIR FOLLOW-UP CARE.

Angela serves as the direct supervisor to the staff nurses on board the Flying Eye Hospital. She works to ensure the smooth running of the clinical area and safe delivery of patient care.

Angela is committed to educating our local partners in patient care and recovery. She loves being able to share her knowledge with partners and members of her nursing team. This exchange of skills is one of the things that makes Orbis programs so effective.

STAN LOVIN

FLIGHT MECHANIC, USA

ABOVE In the belly of the plane, Stan monitors the many hoses and lines that connect clean and sterile air to the operating room.

"I have really enjoyed meeting all of the wonderful people across all of the countries Orbis visits."

TOP The area of the plane that would hold suitcases on a commercial flight serves as an office for Orbis staff while programs are underway.

BOTTOM FedEx-donated units help keep all of the plane's necessary equipment and parts organized.

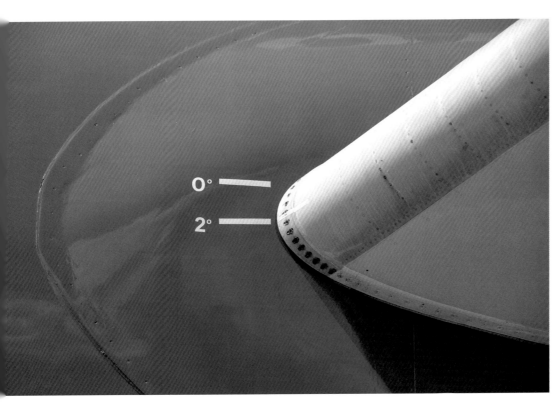

As one of the flight mechanics, Stan flies with and helps maintain the aircraft and all of the ground equipment that supports the Flying Eye Hospital.

The MD-10 plane is entirely self-sufficient, with its own generators, water-purification system and hospital-grade gases. All the team needs on arrival is a runway large enough to accommodate the plane, a water source and, of course, enthusiastic eye care teams to train.

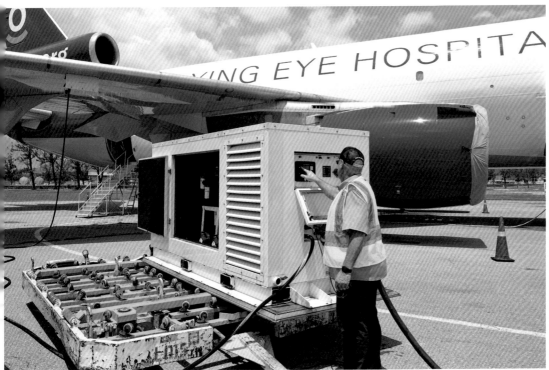

TOP Indicators near the elevator of the plane help ensure the plane is perfectly balanced before takeoff.

BOTTOM Stan monitors the generator that powers the Flying Eye Hospital, making it entirely self-sufficient.

DR. SANDRA JOHNSON

VOLUNTEER FACULTY, GLAUCOMA SPECIALIST, USA

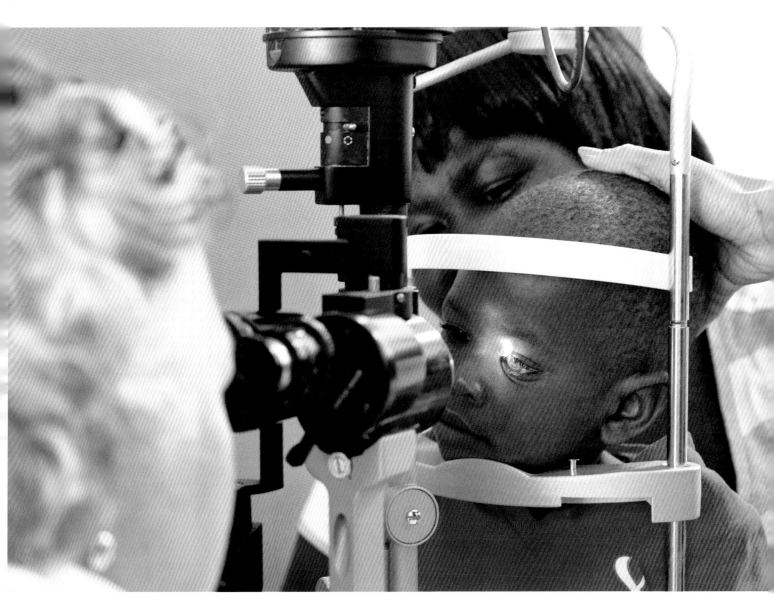

ABOVE Sandra screens a child for pediatric glaucoma.

"The Orbis group really becomes a team on programs – all of us unified by the common mission."

Sandra serves as one of our amazing Volunteer Faculty, with a specific focus on glaucoma. She works to teach as much about glaucoma and glaucoma treatment as possible over the span of a program.

As local partners have varying levels of training, Sandra has to adjust her teaching to meet the needs of the doctors she trains and the patients she sees.

Sandra hopes to leave our partners with both the enthusiasm and the resources to continue their learning and progress in their skills.

We could not achieve our mission without our global force of more than 400 Volunteer Faculty from more than 30 countries who are united in their dedication to teach, train and inspire.

ABOVE The eye care team celebrates after a successful surgery on board the Flying Eye Hospital.

TOP RIGHT Sandra is in surgery mode as she treats a glaucoma patient on board the plane.

RIGHT Sandra leads a lecture on glaucoma for local eye care teams.

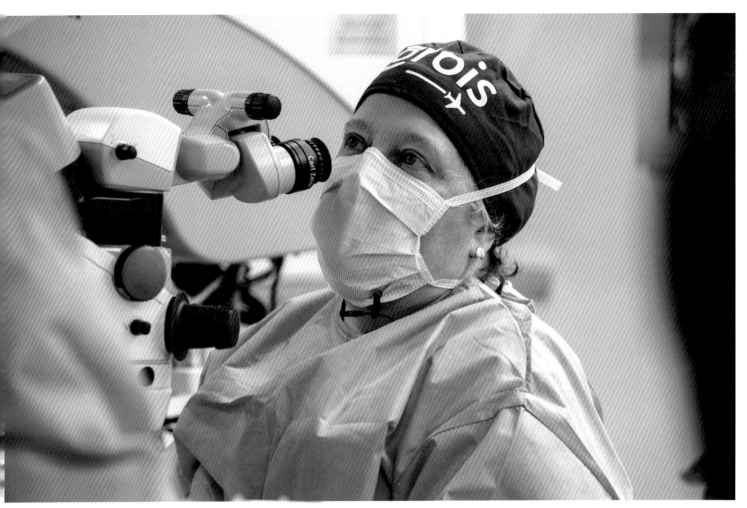

GLAUCOMA IS THE WORLD'S LEADING CAUSE OF IRREVERSIBLE BLINDNESS.

DR. MARIA MONTERO

HEAD OPHTHALMOLOGIST, MEXICO

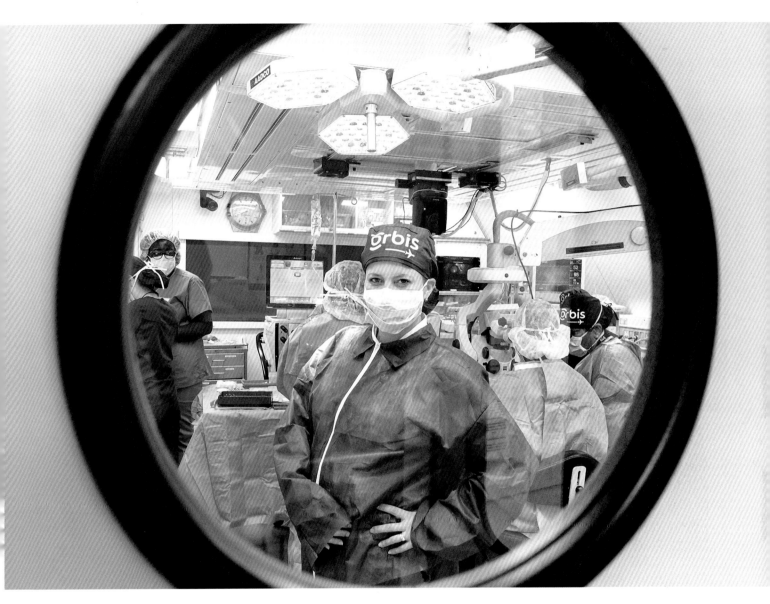

ABOVE Maria prepares for surgery on board the Flying Eye Hospital.

"On my first Orbis program in Bangladesh, doing pediatric post-ops, I got to see the look on children's faces when they realized they could see and the tears falling from their parents' eyes. That was a very special moment."

THE NUMBER OF PEOPLE IN NEED OF EYE CARE IS OUTPACING THE NUMBER OF TRAINED OPHTHALMOLOGISTS.

As the Head of Ophthalmology for the Flying Eye Hospital, Maria oversees all of the ophthalmic content for each program. This includes supervising the planning visits, the programs themselves and the surgical case reviews. Maria also manages the staff ophthalmologists and the Certified Ophthalmic Medical Technologists.

Maria also spends a lot of time making sure patients recover properly with post-operative care. This follow-up is critical in ensuring a patient's full recovery. Maria says it's amazing to see how people's lives are completely changed by the gift of sight, even after just one day.

LEFT Maria helps as local doctors prepare to screen patients.

TOP Maria facilitates discussions as participants watch a live surgery happening on board the Flying Eye Hospital.

BOTTOM RIGHT Maria checks equipment in the state-of-the-art simulation center.

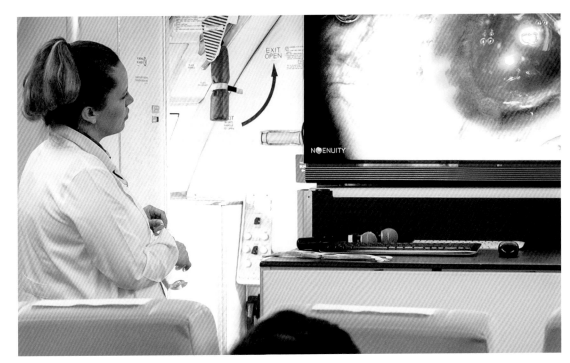

VALERIE SUBERG

SENIOR MANAGER, AIRCRAFT MAINTENANCE, USA

ABOVE Valerie explains her role on the Flying Eye Hospital to FedEx employees receiving a tour of the plane.

"It's truly amazing to see the doctors at work and the patients that were helped by the Orbis team. It's always emotional to see how lives are changed when sight is restored."

TOP Valerie stands next to the left main landing gear under the belly of the Flying Eye Hospital.

BOTTOM The Flying Eye Hospital, an MD-10 aircraft, is so large that it requires three landing gears.

TOP RIGHT Valerie monitors the completely digital cockpit before takeoff.

BOTTOM RIGHT Special equipment helps Valerie monitor and maintain the water tanks that supply the hospital with clean water.

Valerie leads the team that provides aircraft maintenance support for the Orbis MD-10. She is responsible for safely getting the Flying Eye Hospital to its destination so Orbis can deliver hands-on training and sight-saving surgeries.

Before every program, it is also her responsibility to make sure the Flying Eye Hospital meets all hospital requirements for heating and air, water and medical gas. Getting all of this arranged for each program requires a large group effort; the whole team must come together to ensure everything gets done.

THE FLYING EYE HOSPITAL HAS A CUSTOMIZED MODULAR DESIGN THAT ALLOWS THE HOSPITAL SECTION TO BE REMOVED FOR EASY MAINTENANCE.

LEO MERCADO

STAFF NURSE, PHILIPPINES

ABOVE Leo assists in a
surgery at a local hospital.

"I've seen families travel so far to get the sight-
saving treatment they need. Sometimes all
they need is a five-minute laser treatment, and
then the next day, they can see again."

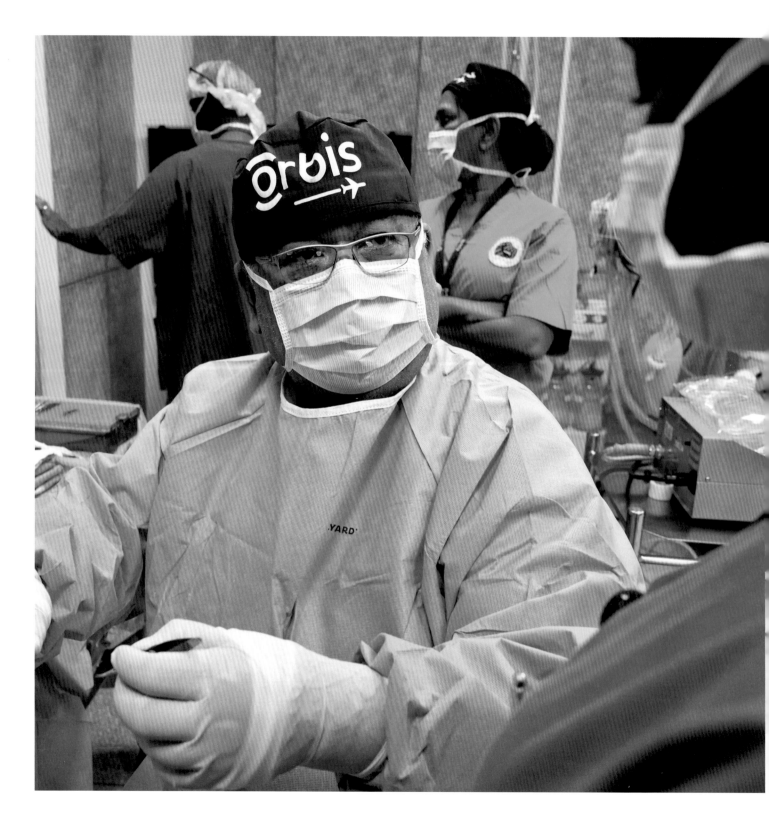

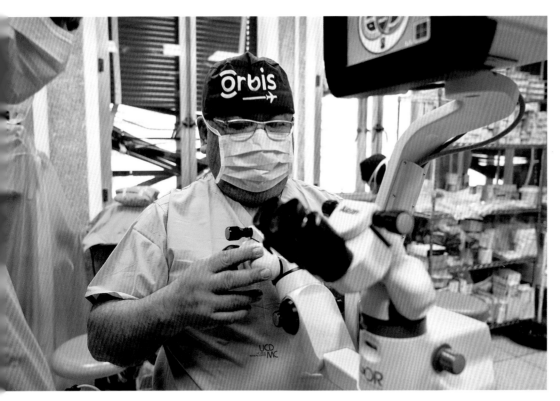

Leo is one of the most seasoned Flying Eye Hospital staff members, with many years' experience working with Orbis. You'll find Leo to be a calming influence in the operating room. He teaches the local nurses how to support the surgical team during surgery, making sure the instruments are prepared and on-hand at a moment's notice. Orbis teaches the whole medical team; professional, efficient nursing is critical in eye care.

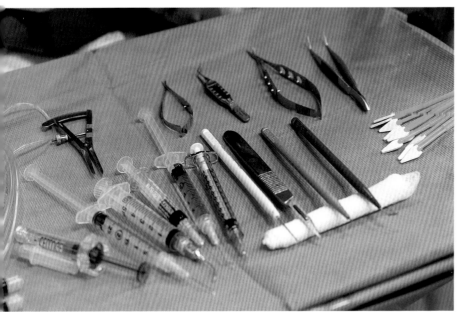

FAR LEFT Leo explains the proper technique for giving medical equipment to a surgeon.

TOP Leo checks the microscopes in the operating room to make sure they're adjusted properly.

LEFT Making sure all surgical tools are sterilized and organized properly is an important part of preparing for surgery.

DR. BRADFORD LEE

VOLUNTEER FACULTY, OCULOPLASTICS, USA

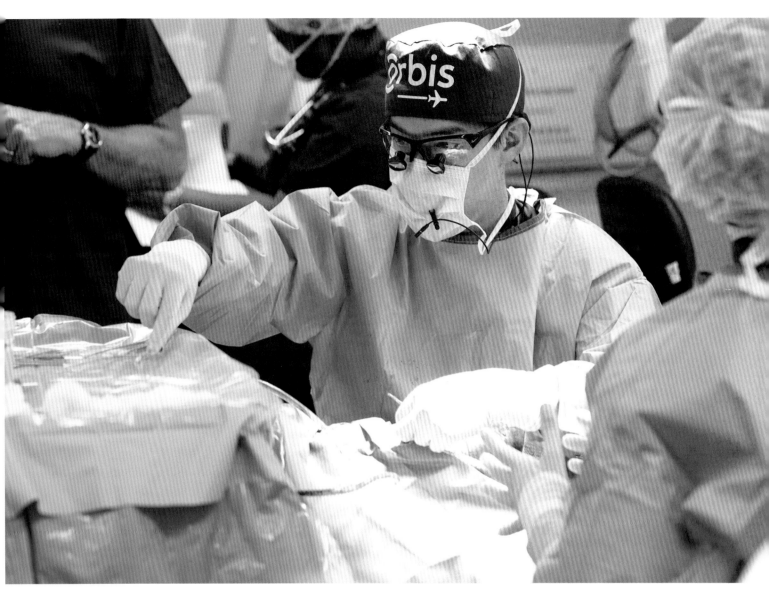

ABOVE Dr. Lee performs surgery on board the Flying Eye Hospital.

"Seeing the excitement of a patient who could finally open his eyes and see again after a traumatic injury was tremendously gratifying."

Dr. Lee serves as another one of our amazing Volunteer Faculty, specializing in oculoplastics. His role includes teaching surgeons hands-on skills in oculoplastics as well as hosting lectures to answer any questions local doctors may have about the topic.

As each country has different rates of conditions that cause blindness and visual impairment, it is imperative that Orbis bring specialists most familiar with the cases each country sees. This ensures that local doctors gain experience and confidence in treating the most common problems in their communities.

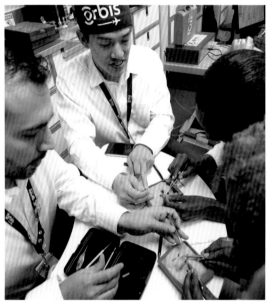

TOP Dr. Lee gives a lecture on oculoplastic surgery in the classroom of the Flying Eye Hospital.

ABOVE Dr. Lee instructs local doctors on proper surgical techniques, using simulation technology.

RIGHT Dr. Lee screens a patient in a local hospital and explains to training participants what he is looking for in the screening process.

ORBIS HAS A CADRE OF OVER 400 WORLD-CLASS VOLUNTEER FACULTY, MEDICAL EXPERTS WHO ARE IMPROVING LIVES BY TRAINING EYE CARE TEAMS IN LOCAL COMMUNITIES.

ALANA CALISE

PROGRAM MANAGER, USA

ABOVE Alana prepares for the first day of surgery during a Flying Eye Hospital program.

"You never forget the patients that are capable of expressing gratitude, joy and glee after having just undergone sight-saving surgeries. To see someone practically jump out of their bed and give hugs of gratitude to anyone in arm's reach is touching."

As the Flying Eye Hospital Program Manager, Alana facilitates the development, implementation and oversight of Orbis's projects all over the world. This involves meticulous planning before every project, coordination with local hospitals and helping patients plan for surgeries, such as arranging their transportation to the Flying Eye Hospital by ambulance.

The Program Manager works to ensure Orbis's ability to fulfill its mission of training ophthalmic care providers to deliver quality eye care for their local communities.

TOP Alana ensures accommodations are provided to all patients who need them.

FAR LEFT Alana works closely with patients and their families to coordinate all travel logistics.

LEFT Alana meets with the local team at an airport to ensure safe arrival for patients.

GLORIA RHOOMES-MUSHORE

STAFF NURSE, JAMAICA & UNITED KINGDOM

ABOVE Gloria checks in with a patient after her operation.

"Following a surgery on the Flying Eye Hospital, a patient I was escorting to a waiting ambulance jumped on me, threw her arms around me and gave me a huge kiss; she was so happy. She came so hard and fast at me that we both almost fell over. I will always remember her."

Gloria works as a nurse in the Flying Eye Hospital's laser room, where patients requiring laser surgeries receive treatment and where local eye care teams can learn about these procedures. She is also responsible for pre- and post-operative care of patients on board the plane.

This job requires a special touch to make patients feel comfortable, especially those who have never had an operation or been on a plane before. Respecting patients and treating them with care is a critical part of making them feel comfortable.

Gloria works to train local nurses in delivering this quality of patient care, teaching them how to be compassionate and empathetic with patients. This extra step in training ensures not only that surgeries on board the Flying Eye Hospital are successful, but also that patients thrive.

LEFT Gloria escorts a patient off the plane after they received treatment on board the Flying Eye Hospital.

ABOVE Gloria goes over surgical plans, including pre- and post-operative care, with training participants.

"THERE ARE FEW OCCASIONS IN LIFE WHEN AN IDEA TAKES OFF AND LEADS TO ACHIEVEMENTS BEYOND OUR WILDEST EXPECTATIONS: WHEN A MISSION IS DRIVEN BY A VISION SO CLEAR AND COMPELLING THAT IT LITERALLY ENABLES OTHERS TO SEE IT TOO. ORBIS IS ONE OF THOSE."

KOFI ANNAN, FORMER UNITED NATIONS SECRETARY-GENERAL

THANK YOU FOR YOUR SUPPORT.

ACKNOWLEDGEMENTS

Orbis would like to thank Nick Wood, whose vision for this book and generous donation of his time and photographs made this project possible. Nick has been a London-based photographer and videographer for more than 35 years. His commissions vary from images of the built environment to natural portraits of people in their places of work or living. Nick has photographed extensively overseas in various locations, from the tropical forests of the Amazon basin to the desert of Arabia. With the dawning of the digital age in photography, Nick conceived and shot an internationally acknowledged series of 360-degree books in London, New York and Paris. Having utilized the gift of sight for many years, Nick is delighted to be able to contribute to this project.

www.nickwoodphoto.com

Orbis would also like to thank Clare Baggaley, who generously donated her time to design this book. Clare has spent 20 years in book publishing as a creative director, an art director, and a book designer. She has worked with publishing houses such as HarperCollins Publishers, Bloomsbury, Dorling Kindersley, Carlton Publishing Group and Quarto Publishing, among others. Clare has also collaborated with global brands and institutions such as HBO's Game of Thrones, The 2012 Summer Olympics, Rugby World Cup, Liverpool F.C., Manchester United F.C., Arsenal F.C., FIFA, the BBC, the RHS, Liberty, Ogilvy, Queen, The Warhol Foundation, National Gallery of Art, The London Eye, Good Housekeeping, and the Walt Disney Company.

www.clarebaggaley.graphics

Orbis would like to thank our incredible Flying Eye Hospital staff, volunteer pilots and Volunteer Faculty – past and present – and all our partners and generous supporters around the world. Our sight-saving work would not be possible without you.

References
Pages 5, 9, 11, 54, 85, 88: Bourne, R et al., Causes of blindness and vision impairment in 2020 and trends over 30 years, and prevalence of avoidable blindness in relation to VISION 2020: the Right to Sight: an analysis for the Global Burden of Disease Study. Lancet Global Health. 2020.

Page 65: PricewaterhouseCoopers and the Fred Hollows Foundation. Investing in Vision – Comparing the Costs and Benefits of Eliminating Avoidable Blindness and Visual Impairment. 2013 Feb.